Also by Cassie Premo Steele

Moon Days
We Heal from Memory
Ruin
My Peace
Easyhard
Shamrock and Lotus

This is how honey runs

by Cassie Premo Steele

ISBN 978-1-936373-04-8

Published in the United States by Unbound Content, LLC, Englewood, NJ.
Cover art: Dana's Orange Vase ©2008, by Philip Mullen.

This is how honey runs

First edition 2010

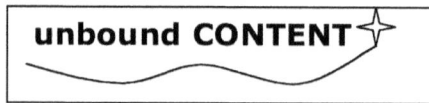

unbound CONTENT

I'd like to dedicate this book to the women poets who have helped me co-create a life of balance and beauty and continue to inspire the people I work with on a daily basis. Anne Sexton, who said it before we did and wasn't afraid of the blood. Audre Lorde, who reminded us that our sun was not the most noteworthy star, only the nearest, and shows us how to take our place equally under that sun. Gloria Anzaldúa, who told us never to give in but to use our many sounding tongues to make a new way. Marge Piercy, who taught us to say "we" so we could be of real use. Alma Luz Villanueva, who opens herself to the dark songs of the planet and lets the deep light shine. Joy Harjo, who sings songs from the dawntime and helps us begin again every morning. Sharon Olds, who broke open the fragile face of motherhood. Alice Walker, who pointed us toward her blue body and said "Sing praises." And Marilou Awiakta, who reminds us that every flower has two faces, one blooming and the other supporting, and encourages us to give and take with respect and balance. I honor you, I thank you, and I pray that you know deep in your hearts how your voices have planted seeds of hope and renewal and healing for generations.

—Cassie Premo Steele

There is no poetry where there are no mistakes, said the next
messenger. I am a human being, I said.
—Joy Harjo, from The Ceremony in *A Map to the Next World*

Table of Contents

Gathering

Before honey runs, it must be gathered. And I did not gather this honey alone. Each of these poems was written for someone else. In my creativity studio that overlooks a wooded creek, I welcome people who want help with their creative process.

Maybe a woman is going through a divorce and remembers how journaling once helped her find her center in the midst of a storm. Maybe someone has a big creative dream in her heart but an even bigger block of fear sitting on her chest. Maybe someone is just lost. Maybe a woman has devoted the last twenty years to her husband, her house, her children and is ready now to let her own self burst forth.

These people come to me, and I create with them.

I call what I do Co-Creating. When they dream, I dream. When they write, I write. When they question, I question. Afterward, I do not ask them to share with me what they've written. And I rarely read what I've written. Instead, the emphasis is on what happens within—the silent dialogue between a creator and her creation. In this way I teach people to stop looking outside themselves for validation, encouragement, recognition, acceptance.

For as long as we are looking outside for these things, we are coming from a place of want, of lack, of emptiness. And we can get to feeling just a wee bit desperate.

And when we are desperate, we'll settle for almost anything.

I call this the vending machine moment of creativity. As we say in the South, "There ain't no honey in that vending machine."

By co-creating together, in quiet space, in nurturing space, in nonjudgmental space, what reawakens is the small voice that says, "Here I am. This is who I am. I am going to be alright." And once we begin to hear that voice within, we start hearing it around us. The trees along the creek might whisper the words of a beloved friend. The dragonfly comes to bend near and encourage us to keep going. The mockingbird reminds us to laugh.

So this is how honey runs. Slowly. With many bees working. With the flowers beckoning. With days of rain that have fed those flowers. With the promise of autumn and seeds falling.

Philip Mullen, the wonderful artist whose painting graces the cover of this book, thinks of his art as a dialogue. He begins the dialogue, but the viewer then joins in. As you page through this book, you will enter a dialogue already in progress. Just as at your birth you entered a world already in progress. Do not mistake this as an excuse for not joining in. You will hear the voices of people I've worked with. You will hear the voices of the poems. You will hear the voices of the wise and natural world.

This is your time to join in.

May your journey be sweet.

—*Cassie Premo Steele*

Co-creating is a process of tapping into each other's senses, taking glimpses of one another's souls, and weaving together strands from one another's lives to create something beautiful together, something that tells both of our stories. Co-creating has always been with us. Creative souls tend to seek and draw one another out because to create fully one cannot work in a vacuum. By allowing others to become part of our creative experience, we invite their light to shine beside our own.

—Amy Alley

Creating

I ride a red horse
but sit backwards.

I watch a blue bird
land on the ground.

I hail a pirate
who is leaving.

I wear snakeskin
I am shedding.

The teacher said
"All growth is letting go."

Wisdom is gained
in losing.

This, I can do.
This, I know.

I've won awards
for losing.

What light

What light do you need to be unafraid?
Start with a candle. Let it light a seed.

Then plant that seed. Give it water.
Walk away. Sleep under the moon.

Soon. What you dream is coming true.
Wake to the sun in the window.

See the seed sprung up. You are that seed.
You are the candle, the moon, the sun.

You are the light. You are the water.
You are no longer afraid. You have begun.

There are 15 ways to create healing

1. ask yourself who you are
2. know there is no right answer
3. listen to the squeaky wheel
4. grease it for once
5. enjoy the silence
6. ask yourself who you will become
7. know there are many answers
8. pick one
9. know you have just begun
10. start over each morning
11. ask a question
12. hear an answer
13. act
14. rest
15. begin again

*Cassie serves as a guide for the lost or wandering
poet resting in each of us, gently prodding us
along the trails we have made for ourselves, but
sometimes have trouble finding. Her greatest tool
is her belief that we all have something unique
and valuable to offer the universe.*
—Cindi Boiter

Better

You tell me you wrote poems in your crazy years
and since getting better, they are gone.
You associate them with vices—
smoking, up all night, so many words, everything too much,
each moment too long.
You are done with all that, you say.

I nod, and turn you around.

Look back, I say. See the seeds you dropped on the ground.
They are blooming into flowers now.

Go back.
Feel the tug on each stem as you pull them.
This is the force of being unattached.
You are like that.
You are your past.
Nothing you did was a waste.
Look, now. You are also a blooming face.

Loss

When you said the word "baby,"
I immediately thought of loss.

I have swum in that whirlpool
under the moon of a frozen season.

I have hid in a cave. I have eaten
seeds not even a crow would scavenge.

I have dug out roots 'til I was bloody.
I have seen tornadoes crossing deserts.

I have moved through the cycles of loss
on the horse of my body. I came back.

Holding a robin's egg

Before dawn, I am holding a robin's egg in my palm,
feeling how its strength is its fragility. How much
longer will it take humans to learn this lesson?

What we fear and call wild is what is in us,
why we stuff our mouths and chop up the dark
with florescence. How much fuller is hunger.

How bright the steady night making its way
toward the dawn. If only we could see how much
is gone. If only we could be this strong.

If only we could feel our feathers
as they start to stir within, the eggs
of our bodies longing to crack open.

Why some ideas don't work out

I am trying to do a planting dance.

With my arms I announce
with my whole heart, Here I am!

I am trying to do a planting.

I want to avoid walking
on my most vulnerable parts.

I am trying to do.

So I wave to everyone, Look at me!
Trying to fly, trying to get high.

I am trying.

I must take the seeds within and stamp
them down with the soft space at my feet.

I am.

There must be seeds.
They must be laid in the ground.

I.

*Cassie was so much a Shaman that I felt a
desire to bring a food offering each time we
met—as an ancient wisdom seeker may have
done years ago with the wise woman in the
temple, the matriarch of awareness.
I was able to find my center, see a path, and
bring it out in reading, meditation, and writing.
This has changed who I am as a person: made me
stronger, more awake, open to healing.*
—Ellen Kline McLeod

This is art

Sky above me, sky within,
my eyes are skies if I let
light in. Light in darkness,
song in silence, color where
once was dim. This is art:
making present what we miss.
A matter of memory.
Wandering. Loss. Going on
at any cost. This is why
we are here: moss
grows under the trees
but not our feet.
We keep moving.
This is what it means
to be human:
it is an acquired art.
It is a presence of heart.
It is the sky singing
and colors falling
and the motion your body
makes while you are
moving, moving, moving
until you depart.

The next step

You ask me how to turn what scares you into what protects
and propels you into the next step.

Look down, I say.

Tiny red toenails like drops of blood fallen from your head
that missed the ground.

See how they grip without holding.
See how they move you forward without forcing.

You paint your toes with blood, I say,
but there are other colors.

Try green. Be growing.
Try pink. Be shy.
Try orange. Be glowing.
Try purple. Be sly.

Try on all the colors that your heart desires
and see where your toes take you.

Turn those tiny toes from tears into rainbows
that grant you luck, wishes, wisdom, and joy.

Discipline is necessary

the body in motion
a line on the page
paint on the canvas

a thing is not a thing
we think it is
we hold to the string

the balloon flies away
we are that balloon
flying through time

when we cling
fearing the discipline
the balloon brings

its breath inside
and pops.
don't pop. breathe, sing.

My Co-Creating sessions always left me feeling open and receptive to possibilities. As a mother with a studio art practice, having someone like Cassie validate and encourage my voice as an intellectually engaged woman and a mother has been empowering. She validated my sneaking suspicion that women are charting new territory in contemporary culture by our methods to collaborate, speak from our experiences, observe subtlety, empathize deeply with others, and maintain a strong head/heart/hand connection. Not only that, but to enjoy the ride of creativity!
—Tina Hirsig

How to ride

Take out your bike
from the cobwebbed basement.
Dust it off.
And go.
See that steep mountain?
That is your road.
There will be places
you can't ride.
Get off and hike.
Sweat if you like.
Swear if it gets too hard.
But keep going.
Soon the road
will lean down
and you will roll.
Feel the wind
on your face.
This is no race,
but if it were,
you'd be winning.
Then you're through.
Happy ending.
Finish line.
Your dreams
and mine
coming true.

How to make magic

The lizards on the western steps warmed themselves
as they waited for you. You were coming from
a long way. You wore witch shoes and I taught you

to get quiet. This is the path you are on.
It is not the only one, though you have been
traveling it most of your life, so it is

the longest. I tell you to turn.
This is why our ears are there, on the side.
To remind us to listen, and to look

in other directions. Not just where we are
going and have been, but around us, at what
shines, what glistens, what catches our attention.

Bold

Athena was not always bold.
We want to think she was.
We want to remember the owl,
the victories, the wisdom.
Nothing comes like this.
The owl was an egg first.
That sound you're hearing.
The one your heart is making.
That is your egg cracking.

Writing is like this

I write with a yellow pen from a place that I have never been.
Writing is like this, I say to you. It will lead you where
you did not know you would go. Desire has nothing
to do with it. The Buddhists are right, I say, at least
when it comes to this. Each word is a stream that pushes
our leaves to a larger river. We learn to swim. Sometimes
we float. Sometimes we sink. Sometimes we rise like salmon
and then turn around and jump back in. It is this easy.
This hard. There is really nothing to it. The only thing is begin.

Yes and no

I am mindful of the way the afternoon light shapes boxes
on the carpeted floor, as if even the sun wants corners
and a space to feel safe in. I am on a limb most days,
reaching in the dark for an apple just beyond my grasp.
Below me is a wheelbarrow. It would catch me if I could,
for once, fall and let the fruit of the world fall into my lap.

A woman who says Yes

She wakes before dawn, remembering her dreams.
She seems to be in them, still, as she rises, halfway
married to someone else, reaching for the tea on
the shelf. While the water heats, she drums her
fingers on the countertop, thinking of the canvas
she stopped working on the day before, anxious
to begin again. Her day goes forward like this.
She moves in her own skin, listening to what sings
within, whispers of dream and desire, bringing to life
what most women fear would set the world on fire.

I have always enjoyed poetry but never had the courage to write a poem. Co-Creating taught me how to journal, react to prompts, and meditate. I have begun to write poems and even sent some to a writing contest. I have learned to tap into my own creativity, to refine the language and nuances of poems I have written.
Co-Creating helped me move from impossible to possible.

—Amy Coquillard

Recipe for the impossible

> You must do the things
>   you think you cannot do.
>   —Eleanor Roosevelt

Here is what to do, my friend,
when your blue anger rises
on yourself: Take a break,
take a shower, go walking
in the rain. Do not let
your brain become a monster.
Use your heart to bake a cake,
take it deep into the forest
in winter, and share it
with the birds there.
Listen to the sweetness
of their songs for you.
You must do the things
you think you cannot do,
I tell you. It is the impossible
that will see you through.

Recipe for a critic

Busy yourself with nothing, aware of the time
that is left. Be content with jars of preserves, made over
and over. Sharpen the tools for cutting wood.
Try a glass of red wine. Leave red orange grass
in a vase without water until it is dead.
Remember that blue night with one distant star?
Don't waste your time reaching that far.
Lay twenty clay pots out for drying, all alike.
What makes you think you are unique?
You are a wallpaper pattern, a pretty decoration.
A chair to sit upon. Slats through which to peek.
Springs under the mattress make sleeping softer,
but no one calls them art. Water from a faucet
is nothing like a waterfall. Everyday objects, glasses,
lipstick, groceries, are provisions, consumable,
repetitive, forgettable. Better yet, don't even start.

Recipe for a muse

Look into a mirror. Paint a yellow sunflower on the side of
your mouth, just above your cheek where memories come out
after centuries in a sandstone cave. See spots of color on the
canvas of your eyes. This is about being becoming seeing.
Frame the moment by putting delicate pink petals around the
next thing you hear until it comes out translated as sunshine.
Do not hide behind your hair or your fear. Your bottom lip
reveals a garden in bloom. Give up sleeping past the edge of
noon. Wake up. Slow it down. Refuse to frown. You are no
strange fish. You belong here. In fact, we hold you dear.
Cultivate patience. Wait in that cave long enough to believe us.
And when you do come out, we will be waiting for you
to show us what you're making with what you've found.

Recipe for the journey

Wipe the windshield so you can see where you are going.
Put your two feet solidly under your hips to open the car door.
Go in. Sit.

Listen to the silence spiral up your spine until it hits your head.
There is nothing to think about here.
Just drive.

Release the break. Roll down hills.
Rules spin past you, unwinding like a snake.
You have all you need. No need to turn back.

But do go in. Deep within. Past the heart, to the back of you.
That core that keeps you going. At the shore of you.
Where gold gleams in your eyes.

Where ocean water beads in your hair.
Keep going.
Do not stop until you get there.

What are you burying?

I am burying my struggle. I created it. I can lay it to rest.
I thought there was a rush, for instance. Now I know more about time.
I thought it was a matter of winning or losing. Now victory is mine.
In order to cover this with dirt, I have to dig back to something earlier.
When my daughter was little, I could be with her without a clock.
This is what I am returning to. My heart. Open. Unlocked.

What are you building?

I am building a book of songs where the pages will never close.
It will lie on coffee tables in every woman's living room and
she will never be lonely because there will always be singing.

I am building a nation of mothers who swirl their drinks
with umbilical cords and tell birth stories during happy hour.
There will be laughter at sunset every night.

I am building a language of children's voices where "to be"
is replaced by "become" and stock markets report on imagination
levels every hour and every fear is drowned by a hum.

I am building a city of families where equal is a daily vow.
No one leaves for money here. Freedom is a given.
Even tears are sweet like milk. Nothing is sour.

When I say we

When I say "we," I mean sisters, women with eyes that have seen
something the same, a vision, a shared notion of what it means
to be sane. I mean an enemy is out there somewhere, your husband,
the media, corporations, the greedy and selfish and rich. But what
would it mean to claim our own power? Who would we be if we
didn't have something to struggle against? I dream of a we
who do not shun sunlight or windstorms or rain or soil on the root.
That is the we I mean. All of us, shedding in fall, baring in winter,
budding in spring, and each and every summer, new fruit.

What I want this poem to do

Take you out, October morning, blue sky igniting,
on the last green grass, and teach you the stillness

of watching for worms. The way the ground gives
clues about what lies underneath. Like your heart

beating differently during fear. I want to make you
kneel in the creek and wait for your eyes to adjust

to deep shadowed light, let you track the footsteps
of raccoons and deer, what came here on the way

to their sleeping places. I want to lie down with you
there, where what is wild does not worry and words

are not necessary because all that is said runs through
the body. I want you to feel the lovely, nonhuman world.

Cassie guided me with her loving presence to begin a new dialogue with myself. It was incredible because she also journeyed as she was guiding me. The power of that is hard to describe, but it affected me profoundly. From the freedom I experienced, a brand new writing appeared.
—Penny Calcina

Let language lead you

You sit across from me with letters in your head.
Your father and mother are dead, in that order.
But this is the thing about death: once it's over,
it doesn't matter in what order it happened.

Poetry is like this: a live child dancing on a grave.
Everything that came before is history to him.
Write down what you remember. Let language
lead you to the bed your grandchildren will lie in.

Praise for the leaving

I want to sing a song of praise for the leaving,
for the bag packed, the tearful goodbye.
I want to frame the beauty of last looks
and longings for one more moment.
I want to share my worship of the road,
the wheel, the train in the distance.
I want to make a triptych of endings.
The solidity of a closed door. The comfort
of night. The resting in letting go.
And in the final note of singing,
I will dance the steps of a new beginning,
the waning moon watching as she does
every morning as the last day goes away.

In Co-Creating I have learned shedding old skin is an idea everyone should embrace. Somehow the human idea of this is confined to becoming bare or naked, but on the contrary, look at the glory of the snake. See what really happens is old skin coming off to reveal a new, better fitting skin.
—Ellen Kline McLeod

S

S is a snake
is the letter for shape
it curls and rolls and reminds me
that every shape is a result of motion and moving
behind me
that I, too, am moving
shedding what is no longer necessary
so I can begin again
in a new skin
skin starts with S, too
and sin
but when we add the K
of kindness and kisses and kids
sin becomes skin
a way of connecting with everything
around us
there is nothing we do not touch
as we move our shapes through the world
like snakes
shifting
yet always remaining
who we are
human
close to the ground
making magic
transformation
one into another
again and again
our bodies
the roads we walk upon
sun after sun after sun

Poem for the last 24 hours of the world

6pm: take a snake in your hand and shake him
'til money falls from his pockets and rains
on the places where bellies are empty tonight.

2am: drag a dragon out of his cave
and light up his mouth, tell him to head south,
burning the liars and dictators and thieves.

10am: sing a morning song to a wren
and ask him to fly on the rays of the sun to the
battlefields and tell them, It's done. No more dying.

4pm: before napping, there's one more thing
to do: go to the zoo and let every animal free.
Tell them to think of all they can do

once we are gone. We humans have had more
than enough time. It's their turn to make this planet
into a place they would want it to be.

How it will begin again

If you want to travel to warm water, you will have to be brave.
There will be a tiny green shoot inside of you growing.
Look at it. Do not be afraid. Trust the tree you are becoming.
Dive into the rain. Open your bag of belongings.
Let them get wet. Already there is an angel.
She is wearing a red hat. She is waving you closer.
She is holding a towel. Take it. It is time.
The world is your carpet. Walk on it.

Celebrate this

laughter is a belly ring
a golden thing
a round halo
around the heart
joy is dependable
we expend it
it comes back again
we are never alone
we breathe in
the presence
of everything
that has ever been
life is a commitment
listen to the ringing
of your own inner voice
singing
this is a new song
of good news

When I was younger, I wrote a lot of poetry, but had turned away from it in the last few years. Working with Cassie, I was able to resurrect my Muse and rediscover the healing and spiritual power of creative mediums. With Cassie as a wonderful mentor, guide, and friend, I have been able to write my way to a deeper understanding of myself. I have fallen in love with writing all over again and allowed creativity to stand as a grounding force in my life.

—Casey Moore

This is how honey runs

This is my release. Be free. This is where the flower grows.
This is what I know. This is as deep as it goes. These are not
just words. When something blooms, it becomes. This is how
honey runs. I am who I am becoming. Smiling is the opposite of
frowning. How high can a dream fly? Your life
can get higher yet. Your dreams are coming true. Swim in
the water that comforts you. There are many shades of blue.
Let yourself play. Who you are is what you are. There is nothing
more to do. Be you. Be you.

Cassie Premo Steele is a Pushcart Prize nominated poet and author of many books and hundreds of poems, essays, and short stories on creativity, healing, and the wisdom of the natural world. She received her PhD from Emory University in 1996 and since then has been writing prolifically and serving as a beloved teacher in university and community settings. In her Co-Creating practice she works with individuals in person and long distance to teach how everyday creativity can help bring about balance, healing, and empowerment. She lives with her family along a creek in Columbia, SC, and can be visited on the web at www.cassiepremosteele.com.

www.ingramcontent.com/pod-product-compliance
Lightning Source LLC
Chambersburg PA
CBHW071751090426
42738CB00011B/2646